CONGRATULATIONS!
You've Just Passed Grade 2

CLARINET

	PIANO PART	CLARINET PART
BLACK BOTTOM	22	10
BLUE MOON	6	3
FIVE FOOT TWO, EYES OF BLUE	28	13
FLYING WITHOUT WINGS	3	1
FROM THE HEART	14	7
FROZEN	10	5
I COULD HAVE DANCED ALL NIGHT	30	14
I'LL BE THERE FOR YOU (THEME FROM 'FRIENDS')	8	4
LITTLE BROWN JUG	33	15
OVER THE RAINBOW	26	12
ROCKIN' AROUND THE CHRISTMAS TREE	4	2
'S WONDERFUL	20	9
THE SHADOW OF YOUR SMILE	12	6
THE SKATERS' WALTZ	17	8
STRANGER ON THE SHORE	34	16
SWAN LAKE	24	11

Exclusive distributors:

International Music Publications Limited: Griffin House, 161 Hammersmith Road, London W6 8BS, England
International Music Publications Germany: Marstallstrasse 8, D-80539 München, Germany
Danmusik: Vognmagergade 7, DK-1120 Cioenhage K, Denmark
Nuova Carisch Srl.: Via Campania 12, San Giuliano Milanese, Milano, Italy
Carisch France, SARL: 20, rue de la Ville-l'Eveque, 75008 Paris, France
Nueva Carisch Espana S.L.: Via Magallenes 25, 28015 Madrid, Spain

Production: Miranda Steel

Music arranged and processed by BARNES MUSIC ENGRAVING Ltd
East Sussex TN22 4HA, England

Cover design by xheight design limited

Published 2000

IMP

International
MUSIC
Publications

International Music Publications Limited
Griffin House 161 Hammersmith Road London W6 8BS England

Flying Without Wings

Words and Music by Steve Mac and Wayne Hector

Rockin' Around The Christmas Tree

Words and Music by Johnny Marks

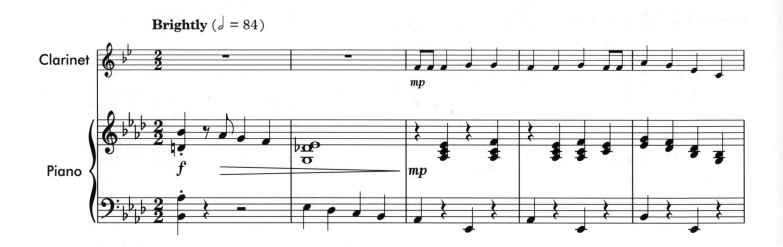

Blue Moon

Music by Richard Rodgers

SPRING CHAMBER CONCERT

PART ONE

Pavane by Arbeau and Theme from Chitty Chitty Bang Bang
Cello ensemble led by Mrs J Reed

Solos

The Entertainer	JOPLIN	Lucy Faulkner
Tomorrow		Melanie Lenahan
Passing Time	RAE	Bansi Patani
You've got a friend	C KING	Charli Lytton
Minuet	HANDEL	Laura Newman
Minuet	MOZART	Holly Levitan
Heaven	BRIAN ADAMS	Sophie Hiller & Charlotte Lane

Ensembles

In an English Country Garden	TRAD	Y7 Instrumentalists
Hava Nasila	ISRAELI TRAD	Y7 & 8 Singers

Rigaudon	HANDEL	Esther Lewinson, Tumi Gbadebo & Mr C Sugden

Solos

Andante	HANDEL	Megan Dos Santos
Elegy	FAURE	Sera Lam

INTERVAL

PART TWO

Solos

Soldier Soldier		Laura Taylor
Memory	LLOYD-WEBBER	Naomi McCarthy
Shadow of Your Smile		Mariam Abuelzein
Here There and Everywhere	LENNON/McCARTNEY	Hannah Thamia
There You'll Be	WARREN	Vicky Thamia
Adagio	J S BACH	Sophie Hiller

C JAM BLUES — performed by the Jazz Group

A Celebration for St. Patrick's Day !

Behind the Bush in the Garden - a traditional tune performed by members of the Senior Orchestra

Flute Reel	Flute Ensemble
O Danny Boy	Year 9 Singers
Shule Agra) Wild Rover)	Chamber Choir

Ensembles

Hayride	NELSON	Jemima Lane & Jessica Warshaw
Jupiter	HOLST	Clara Hobday & Charlotte Rudman

Recorder Ensemble led by Ms E Pallett

Doing Polly's Thing	WISEMAN	Holly Gilbert & Emma Tuttlebury

Please join in the chorus of Wild Rover

CHORUS

And it's no nay never!
No nay never no more
Will I play the Wild Rover
No never no more.

I'll Be There For You
(Theme from 'Friends')

Words and Music by David Crane, Marta Kauffman, Phil Solem, Danny Wilde and Allee Willis

Frozen

Words and Music by Madonna Ciccone and Patrick Leonard

The Shadow Of Your Smile

Music by Johnny Mandel

From The Heart

Words and Music by Diane Warren

The Skaters' Waltz

By Emil Waldteufel

CONGRATULATIONS!

You've Just Passed Grade **2**

CLARINET

Flying Without Wings

Words and Music by Steve Mac and Wayne Hector

Rockin' Around The Christmas Tree

Words and Music by Johnny Marks

Blue Moon

Music by Richard Rodgers

4

I'll Be There For You
(Theme from 'Friends')

Words and Music by David Crane, Marta Kauffman, Phil Solem, Danny Wilde and Allee Willis

Frozen

Words and Music by Madonna Ciccone and Patrick Leonard

The Shadow Of Your Smile

Music by Johnny Mandel

From The Heart

Words and Music by Diane Warren

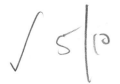

($\boldsymbol{\downarrow}$ = 80)

The Skaters' Waltz

By Emil Waldteufel

'S Wonderful

Music and Lyrics by George Gershwin and Ira Gershwin

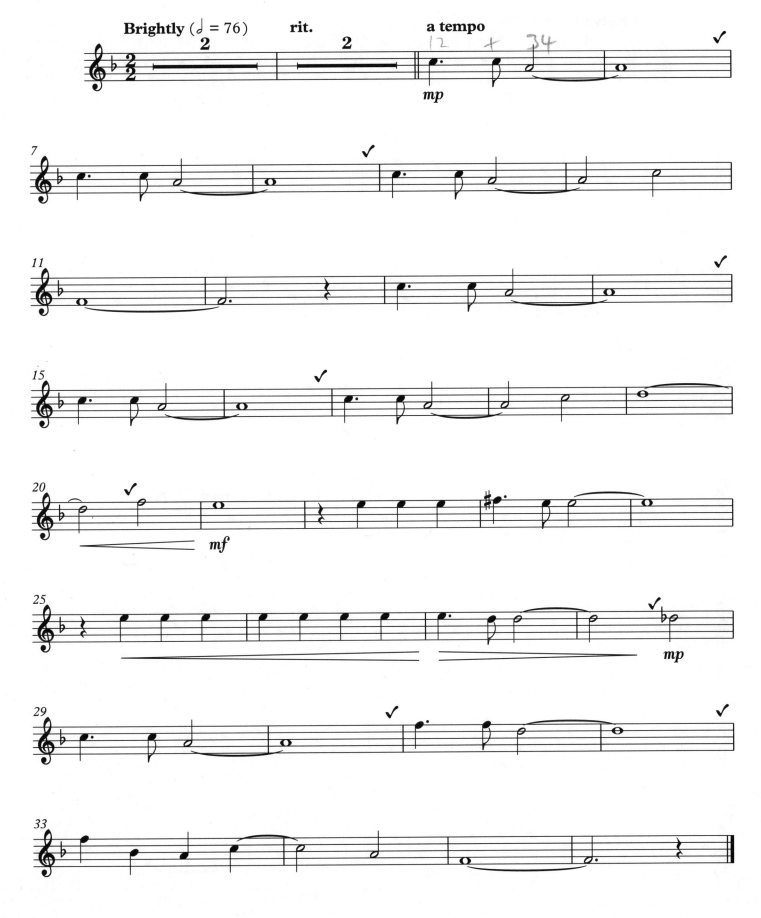

Black Bottom

Music by Ray Henderson

Swan Lake

By Tchaikovsky

long tonguing

×11/5

Over The Rainbow

Music by Harold Arlen

V. Smooth

Reflectively (♩ = 96)

keep R.H on C

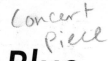

Five Foot Two, Eyes Of Blue

Music by Ray Henderson

With bounce (♩ = 88)

I Could Have Danced All Night

Music by Frederick Loewe

Little Brown Jug

Traditional

Stranger On The Shore

Music by Acker Bilk

Moderately, with feeling ($\quarternote = 84$)

Printed by
Halstan & Co. Ltd., Amersham, Bucks., England

'S Wonderful

Music and Lyrics by George Gershwin and Ira Gershwin

Black Bottom

Music by Ray Henderson

Swan Lake

By Tchaikovsky

Over The Rainbow

Music by Harold Arlen

Five Foot Two, Eyes Of Blue

Music by Ray Henderson

I Could Have Danced All Night

Music by Frederick Loewe

Little Brown Jug

Traditional

Stranger On The Shore

Music by Acker Bilk